GETTING TO KNOW

Hopscotch

PATRICIA HARRIS, PHD

rosen publishing's
**rosen
central**

New York

Published in 2019 by The Rosen Publishing Group, Inc.
29 East 21st Street, New York, NY 10010

Library of Congress Cataloging-in-Publication Data

Names: Harris, Patricia, 1943 October 17– author.
Title: Getting to know Hopscotch / Patricia Harris, Ph.D.
Description: First edition. | New York : Rosen Publishing Group, 2019. | Series: Code power: A teen programmer's guide | Includes bibliographical references and index. | Audience: Grades 5–8.
Identifiers: LCCN 2018006042| ISBN 9781508183679 (library bound) | ISBN 9781508183662 (pbk.)
Subjects: LCSH: Hopscotch (Computer program language)—Juvenile literature. | iPhone (Smartphone)—Programming—Juvenile literature.
Classification: LCC QA76.73.H57 H37 2019 | DDC 005.1/18—dc23
LC record available at https://lccn.loc.gov/2018006042

Manufactured in the United States of America

{ CONTENTS

{ INTROD

$menuclass = 'horiznav'

$topmenuclass ='t

Hopscotch is a block programming language designed for the Apple iPad and iPhone. A block programming language is a language that allows its users to program using prewritten code embedded in shapes that link together like building blocks. Because these languages are easy to use—just drag and drop—users can focus on understanding coding and how computers work while they produce illustrations, animations, and simple games. After a beginner gets good at coding in Hopscotch, he or she can move into learning the vocabulary and syntax of a text-based language, such as JavaScript.

Hopscotch is very good for teaching the fundamentals of computational thinking. This is important because understanding computational thinking can help a beginner think about writing code. What exactly is computational thinking? It does not just mean thinking like a computer—it means more than that. Rather than learning to

```
lecting=false;e.selected=true;e.startselecting=true...
d(a.ui.selectable,{version:"1.8.16"})})}(jQuery)
idget("ui.sortable",a.ui.mouse,{widgetEvent...
t",axis:false,connectWith:false,containment:false
lse,helper:"original",items:")
e,placeholder:false,revert:false,scroll:true,
ions;this.containerCache={};this.element.add...
this.floating=this.items.length?d.axis==="x"||/left|right
items[0].item.css("display")):false;this.offset...
ed").removeData("sortable").unbind(".sortable")
his},_setOption:function(d,c){if(d===
s.options[d]=c;this.widget()[c?"addClass":"removeClass
ype._setOption.apply(this,arguments)),
ptions.disabled||this.options.type=="static"
"sortable-item")==h){e=a(this);return false
a(this.options.handle,e).find("*").andSe
Item=e;this._removeCurrentsFromItems
this;this.refreshPos
his.currentIte
```

think like a computer, coders need to know how a computer processes information before they can write code to make a computer do what they want it to do. An interesting thing about this type of thinking is that it applies to solving everyday problems as well as computer coding problems.

While many organizations talk about computational thinking today, Google has broken it down into four important terms: decomposition, pattern recognition, abstraction, and algorithm design.

Decomposition is breaking a large problem into smaller parts. It is easier to understand how something complex works by looking at its smaller parts. If someone wants to understand how the human body works, for example, the person needs to look at the individual systems within it, such as the lungs and the heart. After understanding how the smaller parts work, it is possible to figure out how they all work together.

Pattern recognition is looking at data—any kind of data—and finding patterns or ways the data seems to be organized. It can mean seeing patterns in how the small parts of a larger program are alike and different. Sometimes, one has to see that no pattern in the data exists; that is also an important part of computer science.

Abstraction is thinking about possible processes that generated the patterns someone can recognize. It also means deciding what information is really important enough to consider. If someone wants to draw a picture of a dog, for example, the person does not need to know what it eats. He or she may know that a dog eats kibble, but that information does not relate to the task of drawing it.

Algorithm design is designing the step-by-step instructions (or algorithms) for solving a problem. Coders needs to know each step and the order in which the steps must happen. If they have a poor algorithm, their program will give poor results. Writing out the steps in basic English phrases—rather than in a coding language—can help someone figure out the steps needed to complete a process. A classic way teachers have sometimes gotten students to think about algorithms is to have them write out the steps for making a peanut butter sandwich and then follow the directions as written. Almost always, the directions have a beginning and an ending, but the middle instructions leave out many important steps. Fixing those directions is an important part of algorithm design.

These are all basic concepts that can apply to any aspect of computer science—and Hopscotch is an excellent tool for beginner programmers who want to learn more about coding and computational thinking.

CHAPTER 1

THE BIRTH OF HOPSCOTCH

All programming is based around solving a big problem using code. Defining that big problem is the first step in thinking like a programmer. This seems like something everyone would think about, but sometimes people sit down and begin to code before they know what the program needs to do. That is a big problem.

THE TIME BEFORE THE CODE

Considering what they know and do not know are other things programmers have to consider. Of course, everyone thinks this way whenever they have a new task to do. In everyday life, most people just seem to know what they know and do not know. For example, think about people getting ready to attend a friend's birthday party. They need to buy a present. With little effort, they consider what they know and do not know about their friend. They know their friend likes video games, but they do not know if their friend has the newest release of their favorite series.

Another thinking activity for programmers is splitting problems into smaller parts, which is decomposition. Programmers who

>> Because many programs are extremely complex, coders have to think about dozens of different objectives, approaches, and methods while they work.

work in companies often work with a team. Each member of the team may have programming skills that other members do not have. So the team breaks a big problem into smaller parts, and then each member may write one or more of the smaller parts of a larger program. When their parts are done, the parts will be put together to make the program. It is important that the team talks about the parts each one is doing—this helps make sure the final product is as good as it should be. Similarly, coders working alone still need to break their programming problem into smaller parts and then link them together at the end.

Programmers must think about the data structures they need. Data structures are ways of organizing data so that the computer can use it. Hopscotch does not allow users to work with this level of sophistication, but it is a thinking skill all coders will need once they explore other programming languages.

Another type of thinking that programmers must use requires testing parts of a program. That involves asking the question: "Is this work really right?" This testing process includes debugging the code for simple errors and making sure each block of code is correct. Good coders test small parts of code before linking them together, and they must also test the whole application when the parts are connected.

These are just some of the many components of computational thinking. Hopscotch not only teaches the basics of block-based programming, it also helps lay a foundation for strong computer science understanding.

BUILDING BLOCKS

Before getting started in Hopscotch, it is important to know a little about who developed the programming language, what inspired its creation, and why the developers wanted to create a new language in the first place.

Hopscotch was mostly created by four people: Jocelyn Leavitt, Samantha John, Liza Conrad, and Rodrigo Tello. Of these four, only Conrad has a deep background in computer science. She was an early worker in an organization called Girls Who Code, which aims to empower girls and women who want to enter the field of computer science. She has also been deeply involved in making programming and computer studies more accessible to kids across the globe. The other three, while not trained as programmers, helped create Hopscotch to achieve a similar goal.

Leavitt was a teacher before starting the Hopscotch movement, and she is highly interested in making tools that can teach kids the coding skills she would have liked to have had when she was young. John started coding when she was in college, and she, like Leavitt, wants to pass along this valuable knowledge to a younger generation. Tello starting experimenting with computers when he was in grade school, but he was educated to become an architect. Similar to the other three major Hopscotch leaders, he wants this programming language to help kids learn how to be creative while also reinforcing computational thinking concepts that will help them—and the world—in the future. While it seems like these four individuals could not be more different, they all want Hopscotch to encourage creative thinking, to help beginners really understand how computer programs work, and to make writing simple programs a task anyone can do.

Hopscotch grew out of another programming language called Scratch, which itself grew out of a language called Logo. Logo is a programming language for education developed in the late 1960s. The name most often associated with Logo is Seymour Papert. Papert was a mathematician and computer scientist at the Massachusetts Institute of Technology (MIT). He had the background one might expect the developer of a language to have, including years of work in complex computer science projects. However, he also had a focus similar to the developers of Hopscotch. He wanted a language that would allow children to learn about technology, engage in computational thinking, and solve problems while using a program they could easily understand. However, he did not have the technology capability that is available today. Unlike Hopscotch, the original Logo language still had to use typed-out words to function. In 2003, MIT, following in the tradition of Papert, introduced Scratch, a programming language based on Logo that uses colorful blocks that can be dragged into a programming area. Using blocks for code meant users no longer had to type lengthy, detailed instructions.

>>BLOCKS AND TEXT

The developers of Hopscotch saw the benefit of using blocks rather than text when introducing coding to new programmers. Text-based programming languages require the user to learn special terms that have special meaning, even if they might seem like normal English words. These languages may also require coders to use special symbols—and sometimes even special spacing—on the screen when typing in code. These actions often result in errors in code that have nothing to do with the thinking that has gone into developing the code. While not perfect, block-based languages help coders think about how their code is going to work, rather than focusing on the technical details of creating it.

OTHER OPTIONS

Hopscotch is just one of many different programming languages. It is not the only block-based coding language, and it is similar to languages such as Scratch, Blocky, and Snap! So why did the developers of Hopscotch want to create a new language? One reason is they wanted to come up with a way to make Scratch even easier to understand. They wanted to remove some of the blocks from Scratch and add some other blocks that would combine some tasks. They also created Hopscotch as a

>> Scratch programming is another good example of a block-based language; the colorful blocks make it easy for beginner coders to see exactly how their choices shape their program.

programming language that is an application on an iPhone or iPad. Scratch and other block-based languages are commonly tied to an internet browser or text editor. Because Hopscotch is an application, the user does not need internet access to use it. Hopscotch and Scratch are still similar, though, because they are good for making simple drawings, animations, and games.

STARTING TO HOPSCOTCH

The first step in starting to experiment and learn with Hopscotch is an obvious one: signing up. Signing up is an easy and free process, and users can even create their own usernames. It is important to come up with a good username. Hopscotch allows people to publish their programs once they are completed, and any game, animation, or drawing published is tied to a username.

After first-time users complete the sign-up process, they are taken to a screen that tells them that they have not completed any projects yet. Also on that screen is a very important button: Get Started. Once users press that button, they are taken to the screen that will allow them to begin a new project. Each new program written in Hopscotch is called a project. It is best for beginners to start from scratch when making their first few programs so they can really understand what they are creating. Then, they just have to tap the plus (+) sign to get their coding adventure underway.

Users are now shown choices for text, shapes, characters, and other options at the bottom of the screen. These choices are easy to navigate by simply swiping in either direction. Once a user has chosen the character they want, such as the space pod, they can select it and start to code with Hopscotch.

Clicking the Add Code button will take users to a screen that is called the When screen. This screen allows users to enter the trigger (the "when") that will start the program after it is written. There are many choices for how a program can start. One common choice is when the iPad or iPhone screen is touched anywhere, the program will start. At the top of the red When box, there is a white box with a square icon in it. Touching the icon will allow the user to choose another icon for that white box. This can be used to, for example, make the program start when someone touches the space pod or another character or button.

The larger white space enclosed in the red box is for adding code to describe what will happen when the program starts.

The When box itself is code and it is not just used to tell what happens at the start of the program. It is possible to have actions taking place in the program and use the When box to tell what happens when a collision takes place between two things on the screen or for another event. One of the options here is for conditionals. That will be explained later.

Before beginners can start adding code to their project, they need to understand what the available code blocks are, how they link, and what the different types of blocks do.

The code blocks fall into six categories: custom, movement, looks and sounds, drawing, variables, and control flow. Most

>> This screenshot shows one of the earliest possible starting screens for a Hopscotch project; there is just one character on the screen, as well as the Add Code button.

programs will use blocks from each of these categories when they are finished.

Custom blocks are blocks that have more than one set of code within a single block. Tapping on the rainbow lines on the side of the block will show what code that block contains. It is important to see what a custom block is doing so changes can be made later down the line. In addition, custom blocks also allow users to create their own new action and name that block.

>>BEGINNER ORIENTATION

When a movement block is used to set a position, coders tells the character where on the screen they want it to go. This is done by using the X (horizontal) and Y (vertical) coordinates to describe the position. This is typically written in parentheses as (X,Y). The exact center of the screen is always X, as the width of the screen divided by two, and Y, as the height of the screen divided by two. The width of the screen depends on the device the user is using Hopscotch on. Because iPads and iPhones are not shaped the same, they have different X and Y minimums and maximums. A general rule for understanding X and Y coordinates is to think of them like this: X is close to zero on the left of the screen, and at its maximum on the right; Y is close to zero on the bottom of the screen, and at its maximum on the top.

Movement blocks allow coders to move their character in many different ways. They can move them forward, flip, or turn; go to a specific place on the screen; set the speed at which the character moves; or set the angle at which the character moves. There is not a block that moves a character backward. When the code tells the character to move forward, it tells the character how far to move. If the distance to move forward is written as a negative number, the character will move backward instead. If the code includes a flip before the negative movement number, the character will actually appear to turn and move in a backward direction.

The best way to learn about these movement blocks is to practice some coding. Open your Hopscotch application, sign in, and launch a new project. Open the character menu and insert a character you like—this example will use a monkey—and click the Add Code button. Select Is Tapped once you get into the When screen. Once you have done that, you will see objects at the bottom; select your character. At the top of the red box, you will now see your character. Click the green arrow to change the screen. To start coding, click on the Go to Center block. The block will move up into your code.

Next, click on the tab at the bottom of the screen for movement. Click the Set Position button. When the Set Position block moves up into your code, do not change any numbers for now. Press the white arrow at the top of the screen to see your code play on the screen. When your character comes up, tap it and see what happens. It will move to the space on your screen in the set position. Now you will want to change the numbers in the Set Position code block to have your character

>> Unlike many advanced programming languages, Hopscotch makes it easy for someone else—like a friend—to quickly look over and help out with a section of code.

go to new places on the screen. To change the number, tap the number in the white area and you will see Select All. When the number is selected, just type in a new number. This number can be whatever you want, starting at zero, but there is an upward maximum, depending on your device. By inputting different number combinations, you will be able to figure out which numbers place your character at different places on the screen. Once you start coding, you will need to be able to put an object anywhere you want.

>>LESSONS IN HOPSCOTCH

You can add other elements to your screen by pressing the home button and choosing your draft. When you do, you will be back on the screen with the plus at the bottom. Just click the plus sign to add a new shape, character, or jungle object. Once you have added whatever additional elements you want, you can position them on the screen by inserting the same code you used for your first character. One thing you will notice as you learn more about Hopscotch is that you will be reusing many ideas and chunks of code as you program. This is an important aspect of computational thinking.

Another important basic set of blocks is control blocks. While movement blocks control the actions of the text, symbols, characters, or jungle elements on a project, control blocks tell the program what it should do. One important control block is Wait. The wait code makes the program stop for a few milliseconds. It is possible to make the wait longer by changing it to a larger number, depending on how long a user wants the program to wait.

To make good use of Hopscotch, users need to combine different blocks to tell their program what to do. Below is an

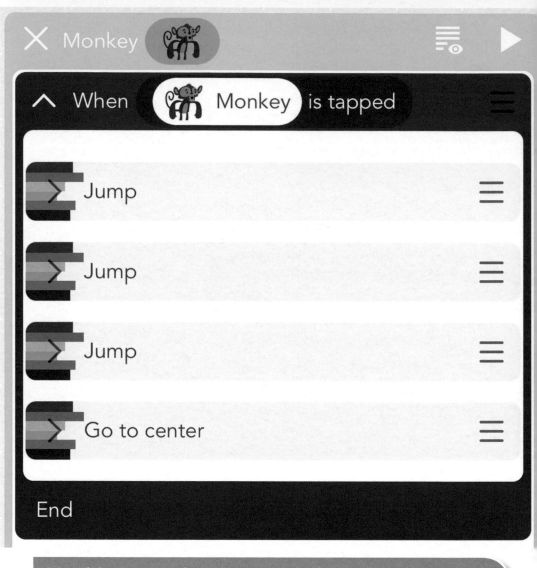

X Monkey

When (Monkey) is tapped

> Jump

> Jump

> Jump

> Go to center

End

>> This screenshot is an example of how to combine custom code blocks. When this program is run, the monkey will jump three times and go to the center of the screen whenever it is tapped by a user.

example of code using different kinds of blocks. There is code for both a monkey and a crocodile. The monkey code uses the custom code for jump, which is just a series of movement codes.

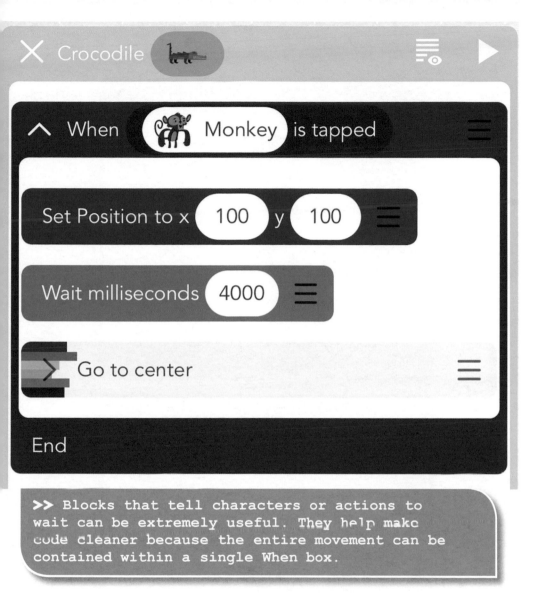

X Crocodile

When Monkey is tapped

Set Position to x 100 y 100

Wait milliseconds 4000

Go to center

End

>> Blocks that tell characters or actions to wait can be extremely useful. They help make code cleaner because the entire movement can be contained within a single When box.

You can create a project with this example code and see what happens. Once you see how that code is working, you can change the monkey code to use another control block: Repeat. Start by deleting the three jump blocks. Then, add in a repeat control block. Change the number from five to three, then run your program. You will see that the action the monkey takes is the same as it did before.

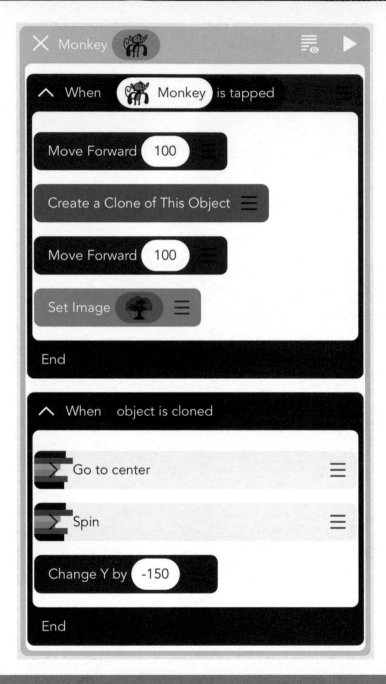

>> With these code blocks, the program will display a monkey sitting underneath a tree—it accomplishes this by using the Create a Clone function effectively.

Repeat is a control block that allows users to group together code that they want to happen more than once in a row. Users simply input the number of times they want that specific portion of code to repeat. In the example of code above, if the number of repeated monkey jumps is set at ten, the crocodile will get to the center before the monkey.

Another control block is Create a Clone. This creates another object identical to the original. If there is a clone, it is possible to give a new set of directions to the original object by changing the When to When Object Is Cloned. The cloned object will do whatever is in the original code, and the original item will do whatever is in the new When box.

Another important class of code blocks is looks. Looks blocks allow users to change how their elements are displayed. The Grow custom block allows an element to get increasingly bigger, up to a set size. It is also possible to set the color of an object with Set Color, which is often used with shapes. Objects can also be changed to look like other objects or sent backward or forward in visibility—that means they can appear and disappear when the coder wants them to.

Draw, another group of blocks in Hopscotch, allows an object to draw a line showing how the object has moved. This is an important feature that can be used to make any kind of drawing a user can imagine. It can also be applied to more advanced applications of Hopscotch.

CHAPTER 3

DRAWING THROUGH CODE

Before coders can create simple drawings, they need to know what they want to create. Then, they need to think about the shapes, characters, or jungle objects they want to use. They also need to think about where they want the items on the screen and if they want to draw some trails. They need to decide on the parts they will need to create the whole and any repeating blocks that might help develop better code. Most of the work in coding is thinking—computational thinking!

Coders might have noticed the drawing choice under Custom on the page where they introduced a character. That is an easy way to draw a picture using tools like those found in any very simple drawing application. However, it is not using coding to make a picture.

If coders want to save their pictures, they must upgrade and become Hopscotch subscribers. They can start a free trial for a week but must have an Apple iTunes account and agree to a charge to get the free week. The subscription gives users access to other tools and lessons as well as allowing one to save. The illustration below is a simple picture using the drawing choice, saved with a screenshot.

>> This scene, which includes several objects, such as a tree, sun, and the ground, is a basic example of how Hopscotch can be used to create drawings.

Publish

>> This screenshot shows an example of using Hopscotch's coding blocks to create a scene similar to the hand-drawn picture on page 27.

While using drawing can be fun, it is not coding and does require a subscription to save the drawing. The picture drawn using coding is not exactly like the one drawn using the drawing tools, but it has the same components. Just like with the drawing tools, Hopscotch users need to know what they are trying to draw and how they can make that artistic vision come to life.

>>THINKING BEFORE CREATING

Here is a Q&A to help you through the thinking that is required in the creation process.

1. What parts are needed to create the whole drawing? For the picture shown, a coder needs the grass, the sky, the sun, and the tree.

2. How will the screen get filled with color? A coder would use code to draw a trail. If an object is drawing a trail, the coder can set the color and width of the trail. The big blocks of blue sky and green grass are wide trails, which means the coder must think about how much of the screen should be covered with each color.

3. How can the items in the drawing be the right size and in the right place? A coder can set the position of objects. Coders will need to recall where different X and Y numbers place an item on the screen. In the example below, the coder will need to think about creating the

(continued on the next page)

(continued from the previous page)

sun and the tree—which are not trails—and the X and Y coordinates for their position on the screen.

4. What shapes, characters, or jungle objects will be included in the drawing? Two characters were used to draw this example picture: the filled circle shape and the tree from the jungle characters. The filled circle shape was used to create the sun. The tree was used to create the trails for the ground and the sky and the tree. If something other than the tree was needed to leave the trails of color, a third object would be needed. That would not be "wrong," but it would suggest that the code could be more streamlined.

When beginning a project, users need to add the two items for drawing onto the screen by choosing to create a blank project and adding the two items with the plus sign at the bottom of the screen. They can then add code for the parts of the drawing. They might select to add code to the filled circle first because the code for the sun is easiest. They would choose when the game starts and set the position, the size, and the color for the sun shape—the filled circle.

Once the code for creating the sun is finished, coders can tap on the lines in the upper right-hand corner of the blue box to go to the blue box for code for the tree. Doing the code for the tree means they must think about the tasks they are asking the tree

>> One of the best parts of programming is finding creative solutions to unique problems—and Hopscotch makes it fun to explore and play around with different blocks of code.

to do: draw the ground, draw the sky, and add the tree to the picture. These tasks can be included in one blue code box for when the game starts. If the Set Invisibility code block is used, and the percent is set to 100, the tree will be hidden while the trails are made and the tree will not be moving across the screen while the code draws the picture.

The Draw a Trail drawing code block would need to be used twice. It is not included in a repeat lock because the variables for color and width will be different. To draw a trail, the X and Y position for the tree need to be set. While the X position can stay the same, the Y position must change. This will put the blue

✕   👁 ▶

∧ Banyan 🌳   ≡

∧ When game starts   ≣

Set Invisibility percent   100   ≡

Set Position to x   50   y   50   ≡

∧ Draw a Trail color ⬭ width   600

    Move Forward   900   ≡

End

Set Position to x   50   y   700   ≡

∧ Draw a Trail color ⬭ width   800

    Move Forward   900

End

Set Position to x   500   y   400   ≡

Set Invisibility percent   0   ≡

End

>> Using this block of code, the Hopscotch program
will use the tree object to paint most of the scene
before it appears to finish things off.

sky at the top of the screen and the green ground at the bottom of the screen. It might take a coder looking at the results of the coding to be sure the X and Y starting points and the trail widths and colors are correct.

During this process, users can press the play button to see what their code is doing. While it may require no changes to get the trail correct, the tree may need a few changes in the Set Position variables to get it where it needs to be. If the tree does not show at the end, for example, it is likely that the Set Invisibility block percent needs to be set to 0. All coders, no matter what language they use, must debug parts of programs as they go along.

While this may seem simple, this drawing can be a great starting point for more advanced uses of Hopscotch, such as animations or more complex scenes.

CHAPTER 4

GET ANIMATED

One thing that makes Hopscotch great is the wide set of tools it gives users. For example, it is possible to use the software to make a simple animation. All a user needs to do is choose a character at the plus sign and give it directions

>> Unlike Scratch and some other block-based programming languages, Hopscotch's wide variety of tools can be used anywhere, on any Apple mobile device.

to follow. Hopscotch makes learning about animation—like coding—much easier for a beginner.

ROBO'S FIRST STEPS

When coders want to animate characters, they often want to start the movement when they tap on specific characters. If they choose the when block for When Is Tapped, which is the default option, their code will execute no matter where the screen is tapped. Coders need to be aware of these types of details so they can get the movement when they want it to happen. What needs to happen is that the screen must be changed to the character before the movement codes are entered.

Because Hopscotch wants to make coding as easy as possible, movement blocks can be included in custom blocks. Custom blocks are special commands that make certain tasks easier. The Go to Center block is one of the custom blocks included in Hopscotch. If the block is moved to the coding space and the rainbow is tapped, the commands included in the custom code will be displayed. Go to Center has one movement command: Set Position to X screen width and Y screen height divided by 2.

The Spin and Jump custom codes are two other blocks with movement commands. Spin has four movement codes and Jump has three. The Go to Finger custom block has only one block of movement code. It is a Set Position block, similar to what is used in the Go to Center command, but it has different positions in the set X and Y boxes. Go to Finger tells the computer to go to the Last Touch position on the screen for each one. If coders use the Go to Finger custom block after they have tapped the character to start some other actions, the character will go to the position where the character was located.

So, using Robo as the character, if When Robo is tapped is used to start the code, Go to Finger sends Robo back to the place where the action started. If the When block Tap Anywhere on the screen is used, Robo would go to whatever place on the screen happened to be tapped to start the program.

COMMANDS ON COMMAND

The other two command codes do not handle movement, which is important to note. The Grow and Change Color commands change how an item looks. Coders can use these two commands to make changes to a shape. The code for Grow has two green codes, but one code is included in a blue code box: the Repeat Times 10 control block. This combination of blocks tells the computer to grow the object by 10 percent for the number of times entered in the oval for the repeat. If the repeat is increased or decreased, the shape will be larger or smaller than the default size.

The Change Color custom block includes a block to set the color and a Wait block from the control commands. This command is to set a random change of color ten times. The Wait code is part of the command so that the user can observe all the color changes as they happen. If there was no Wait, only the first and last color would appear. The computer would work so fast that the colors in between could not be seen on the screen.

>>MOVE IT, MOVE IT

Other movement commands include:
- Flip, which changes the character from facing one direction to facing the other way.
- Turn, which turns the object the number of degrees entered. If a Move Forward block is entered after the turn block, the object will move in the direction it was asked to turn. If the Turn and Move Forward are repeated, the object again turns the specified number of degrees and moves.
- Set Angle, which is somewhat like a turn, but when the Move Forward command is run a second time, the object continues in the direction it was set to go with the specified angle.
- Set Speed, which makes an object move faster or slower on the screen.

The way Hopscotch is structured makes it easy for beginner coders to tie together their drawings and movement blocks to make a real animation.

Putting a scene and some animation together is easy with Hopscotch. Any user can draw a scene with coding blocks, and animating that scene is possible with the simple use of

>> This screenshot shows the scene of a simple animation. With just a few objects—most importantly the dino character—it is possible to make a cool animation.

movement and direction blocks. The concepts introduced in this sample can be used to make an animation with two figures that interact with each other. It is possible to achieve a lot of complexity using the simple tools of Hopscotch. In this scene, a dinosaur is placed next to a tree. Users can create their own unique animations using the features explained below.

ANIMATING LIKE A PROGRAMMER

While creating a drawing like this is easy to do in Hopscotch, animating the scene requires a little computational thinking, or thinking like a programmer. This means users need to think about a few things to get their animation going:

- How to define the problem
- What they know and do not know
- Whether the problem can be split into different parts
- Any reusable parts in the program
- How their data will be structured
- How they will test the parts and the whole of their work

Defining the "problem" here is easy: The scene needs to be animated so that the characters can interact with it. However, when coders consider what they know and do not know, they know they need more details. They need to know specifically where the ground, sky, sun, and tree need to be located and what sizes they need to be. They know they need two characters, but they need details on where the characters should be when, for example, the dinosaur pounces on the monkey. They will also need to develop the skill of adding sound to an animation, which adds another layer of challenge.

This is the kind of thinking that Hopscotch encourages. When the problem is split into parts, coders can know that they need to draw the ground and sky, put in a sun, and have the tree placed in an appropriate spot. Just like in the previous example, the tree—as an invisible object—can be used to draw the background, and then a Set Position code was used to place the tree and make it visible. This code was all included in the tree code, which can be the first part of an animation code. The sun in the drawing is another part of the code. The final part is the code for the dinosaur—the animation's main character.

Unlike many other popular programming languages, such as JavaScript or HTML, it is not easy to reuse code in a block programming language like Hopscotch. This is because coders cannot save items into modules that they store in a library associated with the programming language. However, they can look back at their code to think about the work they did before and how they can use it again. While data structures are also not a part of Hopscotch, coders do need to think about the data they will need to add to code blocks—especially when it comes to wait times.

The last task a programmer must accomplish is testing parts and testing the whole. That is easy to do in Hopscotch. While it is one of a coder's final steps, it is important to check a program multiple times. Often, programmers write code, stop what they are doing, press the play arrow, and see what they have done. When coders think all their coding is complete, they can play their project and see if what happens is what they want.

The code for this example animation is shown on the following pages so you can see how the details fit into the blocks of code.

✕   👁 ▶

⌃ Banyan 🌳   ☰

⌃ When game starts   ☰

Set Invisibility percent `100` ☰

Set Position to x `50` y `50` ☰

⌃ Draw a Trail color ⬤ width `600`

Move Forward `900` ☰

End

Set Position to x `50` y `700` ☰

⌃ Draw a Trail color ⬤ width `800`

Move Forward `900` ☰

End

Set Position to x `500` y `400` ☰

Set Invisibility percent `0` ☰

End

End

⌃ Circle ⬤   ☰

⌃ When game starts   ☰

Set Position to x `50` y `800` ☰

Set Size percent `300` ☰

Set Color ⬤ ☰

End

End

>> This code block, along with the block on the following page, explains how to make this example animation. This block focuses on the tree object in the scene.

X Dino [icon]   ≡◉ ▶

∧ When game starts   ≡

Wait milliseconds 2000 ≡

> Go to center   ≡

∧ Grow   ≡

∧ Repeat times 7   ≡

Grow by percent 10 ≡

End

End

Move Forward 90 ≡

Wait milliseconds 5000 ≡

Set Speed to 500 ≡

>> This code block, along with the block on the previous page, explains how to make this example animation. This block focuses on the dino character in the scene.

42

If someone knows how to make drawings and animations in Hopscotch, he or she is only a few steps away from being able to make a playable video game. After all, video games are really just animations that allow a user to interact with them. As a result, the difference in code between an animation and a game is that which allows users to input commands and see the results.

Luckily, Hopscotch's design allows users to apply some basic computational logic to their animation and extend it into a functional video game. Some important parts of that process are:

1. Adding text for directions
2. Adding text arrows to the game to cause items to move
3. Causing an action to happen when another action happens
4. Making a new custom block
5. Creating clones
6. Using Clone index
7. Using When Object Is Cloned
8. Using When Self Is Tapped

By combining these commands and options in different ways, even beginner coders can add new elements, such as a directional pad for user input, collision detection for when two characters touch, and other features commonly found in modern video games.

CHAPTER 5

HOPSCOTCH AND FRIENDS

T he creators of Hopscotch had a difficult goal in mind when they created the language: They wanted to make programming more accessible to beginners. Because of that, the language has a lot of support from the coding community, and the skills learned in Hopscotch can easily be translated into dozens of other programming languages with more robust feature sets, such as HTML and JavaScript. These two languages are among the most popular in the world, with billions of people using and interacting with them both on a daily basis.

SKILLS AND THRILLS

Many professional programmers believe one of the best, most exciting parts of coding is the chance to look at a problem, break it down, and come up with a creative solution. No matter the era—from the 1950s, when the first programming language was written, to today—the ability to problem solve has been the most important skill in a coder's toolbox. When faced with real-world development challenges, coders are often given a goal (making a website display a confirmation message when a user submits his

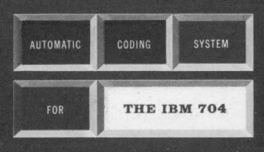

PROGRAMMER'S REFERENCE MANUAL

Fortran

AUTOMATIC CODING SYSTEM

FOR THE IBM 704

>> Developed in the 1950s, the Fortran programming language is the father of all coding languages. It paved the way for many amazing modern programming languages.

or her username, for example) and nothing else. It is their job to search out the best way to accomplish that goal. They might be able to write a block of code in an hour that can accomplish that task, but the true programmer's spirit is to keep attacking the problem until they have found the most efficient way to solve it.

For a lot of computer scientists, that is what is so exciting about the digital world. Unlike in many other fields of study, a coding problem rarely has a single "correct" answer. Even with a simple language, such as Hopscotch, there are many different ways to accomplish the exact same task. Even the examples in this book are not the "correct" way to accomplish a task; another coder might look at the same task and come up with a very different set of instructions. However, while there are no "correct" ways to code, there are certainly more efficient ways. If two programs solve the exact same problem, but one is twice as long, the shorter code is more efficient. Balancing a level of efficiency and power is something most programming languages—and programmers—work hard to accomplish.

EXPANDING ON HOPSCOTCH

Hopscotch is a coding kit that is used to teach coding to younger users or beginners. Because it is so simple to learn and use, however, it is not used for very much outside of schools or amateur hobbyists. To some people, this lack of widespread use might seem like a problem. After all, why would someone learn a language that is not useful outside of itself? However, Hopscotch is valuable not for what it is capable of programming, but what it is capable of teaching.

No matter how long someone has been around computers or programming, everyone always relies on his or her computational thinking skills. The only way to make a computer do what one wants is to understand what the computer actually needs to know. For that reason, Hopscotch is a tool worth much more than what it is capable of actually coding. Any person could search around online for the code for a simple game, copy it, and paste it into a programming language. By doing this, that person would have a game—but what did he or she learn? Would that coder be able to make that game on his or her own?

What Hopscotch does is much more useful for someone who is seriously interested in understanding computer science. Rather than throwing out a bunch of complex or intimidating vocabulary, Hopscotch uses words and blocks that make sense to an average user. In many ways, the language is very similar to pseudocode. Used by both beginners and veterans, pseudocode is basically a detailed outline of what they want their code to accomplish. It falls somewhere in between a regular human language, such as English, and a real coding language, such as JavaScript. There is no set of rules that pseudocode must follow; it is kind of like a rough draft for a school assignment. Though the ideas of the draft probably make it into the final product, the exact language changes.

Hopscotch's similarity to pseudocode is one of its major strengths. Users do not have to focus on making sure they are using the correct vocabulary, and there is no worry that they will misplace a comma and ruin their entire block of code. Instead, they are allowed to focus on the outline of what they want their

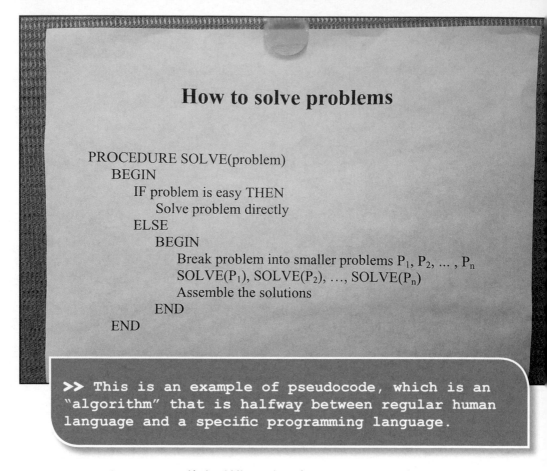

How to solve problems

```
PROCEDURE SOLVE(problem)
    BEGIN
        IF problem is easy THEN
            Solve problem directly
        ELSE
        BEGIN
            Break problem into smaller problems P₁, P₂, ... , Pₙ
            SOLVE(P₁), SOLVE(P₂), ..., SOLVE(Pₙ)
            Assemble the solutions
        END
    END
```

>> This is an example of pseudocode, which is an "algorithm" that is halfway between regular human language and a specific programming language.

program to accomplish. When beginners are ready to move on to a more complex language, such as HTML or JavaScript, they will understand the basics of programming because of the relaxed style of learning through Hopscotch.

MORE LANGUAGES, MORE POSSIBILITIES

Though Hopscotch is an extremely valuable tool for beginner coders, it is also relatively weak. While Hopscotch excels at making simple animations, more complex languages, such as HTML and JavaScript, are needed to accomplish major software development goals.

HTML, which stands for Hypertext Markup Language, is a popular tool for developing websites. It can be run by pretty much any computer without any additional software installation, and its syntax is relatively simple and close to English. In any programming language, syntax means the sets of rules that coders must follow for their code to be understood. While some languages use exotic symbols and confusing abbreviations, the syntax of HTML is much more familiar to an English-speaking programmer. Despite how user-friendly HTML can be, it is still a powerful language for developing websites—something that Hopscotch cannot do. HTML allows a savvy coder to create complex designs, insert images, and provide hyperlinks, which can take users to other webpages with a single click.

For adventurous programmers who want to look beyond website design, it is also possible to use HTML to create simple games. Though no one will confuse an HTML game with the latest blockbuster release for home consoles, even beginners are capable of making an interactive page to entertain their friends. HTML can do many things that Hopscotch cannot, and it is a great stepping-stone to learning even more complex and useful programming languages. One of the most popular programming languages in the world—JavaScript—can use the basics taught through Hopscotch to allow a fledgling coder to accomplish great things.

There are billions of websites in the world. From video game forums to online shopping to government pages, there is a website

>> There is no question that JavaScript code looks more intimidating than Hopscotch's, but the skills learned in Hopscotch can be applied to JavaScript.

out there for everything imaginable. According to a World Wide Web Technology Surveys study in 2018, around 95 percent of each of these websites used JavaScript. Because of this unbelievably high demand, coders with extensive knowledge of JavaScript are highly valued by countless businesses. Just like with HTML, Hopscotch can lay the foundation for a strong understanding of JavaScript. Though the syntax of JavaScript is more complex than Hopscotch, it is also much more powerful. By using some of the same basic concepts—such as knowing how to tell the program to respond to user input—taught through Hopscotch, a JavaScript coder can add an impressive amount of interactivity to a website or another piece of software. It is used by billions of internet users every day for a reason—it is sleek and powerful and has endless possibilities.

JavaScript is a versatile language. It is not only used widely in web design, it can also be used

>> *Minecraft* is one of the world's most popular games, and it can be modified—with anything from new skins to new maps—with JavaScript code.

to make video games. Though it was not created for this purpose, the language is still fast and efficient enough to allow coders to make interactive animations and allow for a player's input. Even more impressive, JavaScript can be used to create customized modifications (or mods) for *Minecraft.* *The Minecraft* modding community loves to spice the game up by adding new levels and monsters, personalized dungeons, and anything else they can imagine—and a popular language for writing those mods is JavaScript.

HOPPING FORWARD

Though it has been around since the 1950s, the world of coding can still be intimidating for a newcomer, whether old or young. That is a shame, because learning programming early can lead to an extremely successful and rewarding career. Hopscotch hopes to help beginner coders approach computer science with no fears and an enthusiasm to make great things through code. Though the programs Hopscotch is capable of supporting are basic, such as an animation or simple game, the lessons it can teach on computational thinking can be carried across to dozens of other programming languages, including some of the most popular in the world.

ALGORITHM A set of step-by-step rules or procedures to be followed to solve problems, especially used in computer programming and math.

ANIMATION A production in which still objects are made to look like they are moving.

BLOCK PROGRAMMING LANGUAGE A programming language that allows you to program using code embedded in blocks that link together.

BROWSER A computer graphical user interface that is used to navigate the web or run applications. Hopscotch is a program used in a browser.

CLONE In computer languages, producing an object that is just like the original item. In Hopscotch, the clone or clones, rather than the original item, will follow the directions that are given after the cloning.

CODE Instructions given to a computer.

COLLISION Two or more items bumping each other.

COMPUTATIONAL THINKING Knowing how a computer processes information so this skill can be applied to programming a computer or solving problems in life.

CONDITIONAL A statement in a computer language that results in different actions based on the outcome of a question being true or false.

CONTROL BLOCKS Code in a computer program that tells the computer what to do.

EMBEDDED Included inside something else, often not seen.

GENERATE To create or make something.

ICON A picture or graphic symbol on a computer screen.

LIBRARY In a programming language, a library is a special set of files, often called modules, stored in a place where they can be found to be used again when coding.

LOGO A programming language that uses simple code to move a cursor on the screen that can draw images or just move across the screen.

MODULE In programming languages, a set of code that can be inserted into code that is being written to do a task that has been done before.

MOVEMENT COMMANDS Code that lets items on the screen move for animations.

SCENE In Hopscotch, this is the background behind your animation or game.

TRAIL A line left behind as an icon moves on the screen.

Canada Learning Code

https://www.canadalearningcode.ca

This organization supports technology learning for all groups, especially those generally underrepresented in technology use.

Code.org

https://code.org

This is a nonprofit organization that focuses on increasing access and the level of computer instruction in schools. It sponsors Hour of Code, an international effort introducing coding in schools.

Girls Who Code

https://girlswhocode.com

This organization is interested in furthering the work of girls in coding. It has supported the writing of books on coding for girls and runs camps.

Hopscotch Company

https://www.gethopscotch.com

This site connects users to Hopscotch.

Kids & Code

http://www.kidsandcode.org

Kids & Code is a nonprofit organization that works to bring computer programming to school children in Canada.

MIT Education

https://scratch.mit.edu

This organization has a commitment to making computer programming accessible to all. It invented Scratch and maintains the website for the program.

One Laptop

http://one.laptop.org

Located in Miami, Florida, this organization reaches out worldwide to bring connected laptops to youth who would otherwise not have access to computers.

FOR FURTHER READING

Harris, Patricia. *Gareth's Guide to Becoming a Rock Star Coder*. New York, NY: Gareth Stevens Publishing, 2018.

Harris, Patricia. *Understanding Coding Through Debugging*. New York, NY: PowerKids Press, 2017.

Harris, Patricia. *Understanding Coding Using Conditionals*. New York, NY: PowerKids Press, 2017.

Harris, Patricia. *What Are Programs and Applications?* New York, NY: PowerKids Press, 2017.

Hutt, Sarah. *Code It! Create It! Ideas and Inspiration for Coding*. New York, NY: Penguin Workshop, 2017.

McManus, Sean. *How to Code in 10 Easy Lessons: Learn How to Design and Code Your Very Own Computer Game*. Lake Forest, CA: Walter Foster Jr., 2015.

Payment, Simone. *Getting to Know Python* (Code Power: A Teen Programmer's Guide). New York, NY: Rosen, 2015.

Woodcock, Jon. *Coding Games in Scratch*. London, UK: DK Children. 2015.

Braatz, Tracy. "Hopscotch: Coding For Kids, A Visual Programming Language." BestAppsforKids, February 7, 2014. https://www.bestappsforkids.com/2014/hopscotch-coding-for-kids-a-visual-programming-language.

Brokaw, Alex. "Hopscotch's visual coding app is now on the iPhone." The Verge, May 12, 2016. https://www.theverge.com/.../hopscotch-iphone-programming-app-available.

Doyle, Matt. "Your Kid's Coding Skills Will Leap Ahead with Hopscotch!" Brightpips, June 10, 2014. www.brightpips.com/your-kids-coding-skills-will-leap-ahead-with-hopscotch.

Harris, Patricia. *Understanding Coding Like a Programmer.* New York, NY: PowerKids Press, 2017.

Harris, Patricia. *Understanding Coding Using Conditionals.* New York, NY: PowerKids Press, 2017.

Harris, Patricia. *Understanding Coding with Hopscotch.* New York, NY: PowerKids Press, 2016.

Harris, Patricia. *What Are Programs and Applications?* New York, NY: PowerKids Press, 2017.

Hopscotch. "About Hopscotch." Hopscotch. http://www.gethopscotch.com/about. Retrieved May 3, 2018.

"Hopscotch Curriculum: Learn to Code—Make Cool Stuff." Hopscotch. http://hopscotch-curriculum-files.s3.amazonaws.com/Hopscotch%20Curriculum%202015.pdf. Retrieved May 3, 2018.

Patterson, Sam. *Programming in the Primary Grades: Beyond the Hour of Code.* Lanham, MD: Rowman and Littlefield, 2016.

Stinson, Elizabeth. "Hopscotch Teaches Kids to Code Without That Pesky Command Line." *Wired*, May 26, 2016. https://www.wired.com/2016/05hopscotch-teaches-kids-code-without-command-line.

Tech Will Save Us. "Know your Scratch from your Hopscotch." https://www.techwillsaveus.com/blog/know-your-scratch-from-your-bee-bot. Retrieved May 3, 2018.

Usage of JavaScript for Websites. Web Technology Surveys. https://w3techs.com/technologies/details/cp-javascript/all/all. Retrieved May 3, 2018.

INDEX

A

abstraction, 6
Add Code button, 16, 19, 30
algorithm, design, 6, 7
animations, 4, 14, 15, 33, 34,
    35, 37, 39, 43, 48–49
 code for, 40
 interactive, 53

B

block programming language, 4,
    10, 13, 14, 40
blocks, 10, 13, 16, 18, 19–20,
    21–22, 25, 29, 31, 33, 35,
    37, 39, 46, 47
 building, 4, 10–12
 control, 21, 23, 25, 36
 custom, 16, 18, 25, 35, 36, 43
 direction, 37, 39
 Go to Center, 19, 35
 jump, 23
 looks, 16, 25
 movement, 16, 18, 19, 21,
    35, 37
 repeating, 26
 Set Position, 19, 35
browser, 14

C

Change Color code, 36
characters, 16, 18, 19–20, 21,
    26, 30, 34, 35, 36, 37, 39,
    40, 43
clone, 25, 43
collision, 16, 43
computational thinking, 4, 6,
    7, 10, 11–12, 21, 26, 39,
    47, 53
conditionals, 16
Conrad, Liza, 10
control blocks, 21, 23, 25, 36
coordinates, 18, 29–30
Create a Clone, 25

D

debugging, 10, 33
decomposition, 6, 8
drawings, 6, 14, 15, 16, 25,
    37, 39, 40, 43
 through code, 26, 29–31, 33

F

Flip, 19, 37

G

games, 4, 8, 14, 15, 30, 31,
    43, 47, 49, 51, 53
Girls Who Code, 10
Google, 6
Go to Finger, 35–36

H

HTML (Hypertext Markup
    Language), 40, 44, 48–49, 51

ABOUT THE AUTHOR

Patricia Harris has a PhD and has taught computer applications and programming in public schools, an engineering college, and universities. She is a self-taught programmer and uses many applications on her computers and iPhone. She has published numerous books with Rosen on computational thinking and coding. Her most recent teaching project has been teaching kindergarteners about coding to run a robot with simple forward, turn, and function commands.

PHOTO CREDITS